CENGAGE Learning

Novels for Students, Volume 5 Copyright Notice

Copyright © 1999

Gale Research
27500 Drake Rd.
Farmington Hills, MI 48331-3535

ISBN 0-7876-2115-3
ISSN 1094-3552

Printed in the United States of America.
1 0 9 8 7 6 5 4 3

The Sun Also Rises

Ernest Hemingway 1926

Introduction

Ernest Hemingway's first novel, *The Sun Also Rises*,
remains, as F. Scott Fitzgerald said, "a romance and
a guidebook." It also became, in the words of critic
Sibbie O'Sullivan, "a modern-day courtesy book on
how to behave in the waste land Europe had become
after the Great War." *The Sun Also Rises*
successfully portrays its characters as survivors of a
"lost generation." In addition, the novel was the
most modern an American author had yet produced,
and the ease with which it could be read endeared it
to many. But for all its apparent simplicity, the
novel's innovation lay in its ironic style that
interjected complex themes without being didactic.

Generally, the novel is considered to be Hemingway's most satisfying work.

The material for the novel resulted from a journey Hemingway made with his first wife, Hadley Richardson, and several friends to Pamplona, Spain, in 1925. Among them was Lady Duff Twysden, a beautiful socialite with whom Hemingway was in love (the inspiration for the novel's Lady Brett Ashley). There was also a Jewish novelist and boxer named Harold Loeb (source of Robert Cohn) whom Hemingway threatened after learning that he and Lady Duff had had an affair. Lady Duff's companion was a bankrupt Briton (like Mike Campbell). The trip ended poorly when Lady Duff and her companion left their bills unpaid. The ending of the novel is only slightly more tragic, yet it recovers those precious values which make life livable in a war-wearied world: friendship, stoicism, and natural grace.

Author Biography

One of the greatest authors of American literature, Hemingway had modest beginnings in the town of Oak Park, Illinois, where he was born to Dr. Clarence and Grace Hall Hemingway in 1899. Young Hemingway pursued sports with his father and arts with his mother without distinction. In 1917, after graduating from high school, he took a junior position at the *Kansas City Star* where he was given a reporter's stylebook that demanded brief, declarative, and direct sentences. Hemingway became the master of this style and adapted it to literary demands.

In 1918 he volunteered for service in World War I and served as an ambulance driver on the Italian front. This experience later served as the source material for *A Farewell to Arms.* His legs were wounded and he was sent home. His convalescence took place over several months at the family cabin in Michigan. When he recovered, he took a position as companion to a disabled boy in Toronto in 1920. There, he again entered the world of writing through the *Toronto Star.* After marriage to Hadley Richardson, he became a Parisian correspondent with the paper.

He and his wife left for Paris where Hemingway associated with those known as the "Lost Generation" (James Joyce, Ezra Pound, Gertrude Stein, and Ford Madox Ford). His first publishing success was a short story entitled "My Old Man" in 1923. For the next few years he continued to meet literary figures (F. Scott Fitzgerald among others) and edited a journal with Ford Madox Ford. In 1925 he began work on *The Sun Also Rises* which reflected his life in Paris among the "Lost Generation." He also wrote *The Torrents of Spring* at the same time. Both were published the following year.

With the success of *A Farewell to Arms* in 1929, Hemingway traveled quite a bit. He frequented Cuba, Florida, and France, contributed money for ambulance service in the Spanish Civil war, and also covered the war for *The North American Newspaper Alliance.* In 1940 he married his third wife, Martha Gellhorn, and published *For Whom the Bell Tolls.* Hemingway and Gellhorn then went to China where he became a war correspondent with the United States Fourth Infantry Division. There he met Mary Welsh, whom he married in 1945.

Hemingway continued to publish until 1952 when *The Old Man and the Sea* crowned his extraordinary career. He received the Pulitzer Prize in 1953 for this story. Unfortunately, by the mid-1950s his adventurous life had taken its toll. Hemingway became depressed and spent time in various hospitals. Finally, he returned from a stay in the Mayo Clinic on June 30, 1961, to his home in Ketchum, Idaho. There he used a favorite gun to commit suicide on July 2.

Book I

The Sun Also Rises is set in Paris and Spain in the 1920s and depicts the lives of a group of young American and English expatriates living in the aftermath of World War I. Often read as a representation of the now familiar "Lost Generation," Hemingway's story revolves around the impossible love affair between the war-damaged American journalist Jake Barnes, the novel's narrator, and Lady Brett Ashley, a former nurse in a hospital Jake was in during the war.

Jake begins his narrative by introducing Robert Cohn, one of his friends in Paris. A one-time boxing champion at Princeton, Cohn, as he is generally called, is now the author of a rather "poor novel" and is living in Europe with his fiancee, Frances. Lamenting the fact that his life is quickly passing by and that he is not really living it, Cohn tries to recruit Jake for a voyage to South America. Jake, however, will not join him. He knows first-hand that traveling to another country does not make a difference and tells his friend that "you can't get away from yourself by moving from one place to another."

Shortly after parting from Cohn, Jake picks up a prostitute walking in front of a cafe. He buys her a drink and takes her out to dinner. Riding in a cab to the restaurant, the girl, Georgette, touches Jake but he pushes her away. He later explains that he was wounded during the war. After dinner, they go to a club where several of Jake's friends have gathered. When Brett arrives, Jake notices that Cohn cannot keep his eyes off her. Jake and Brett soon leave the club and find a cab. As they drive, Jake kisses Brett but she turns away. She tells him that she loves him but cannot bear to go through "that hell again."

They proceed to the Cafe Select and are introduced to Count Mippipopolous, a man who, Brett later confirms, is "quite one of us." Jake leaves early and returns home. As he prepares for bed, he undresses and looks at himself in the mirror. "Of all the ways to be wounded," he thinks. Unable to sleep, he thinks of his accident and how he would probably never have minded had he never met Brett. He cries and finally falls asleep.

The next day, Cohn tells Jake that he might be in love with Brett. When asked what he know's about her, Jake tells him that Brett is a drunk and that she is engaged to Mike Campbell, presently is Scotland. That evening, Jake receives a visit from Brett and the Count. He is feeling "pretty rotten" and Brett sends the Count on an errand so they can be alone. Jake asks Brett if they could live together but she tells him that she would just *"tromper"* him with everyone. She then announces that she is going to San Sebastian and that, when she returns, Mike will be back.

When the Count returns from his errand, they finish off three bottles of champagne and go out for dinner. After some dancing at Zelli's, Brett tells Jake that she is feeling miserable and would like to leave. Immediately, Jake gets the feeling that he is going through something that has happened before. They bid goodnight to the Count and leave together. Outside her hotel, Brett tells Jake not to come up. They kiss, Brett pushes Jake away and they kiss again. Brett then turns and enters the hotel.

Book II

Jake does not see Brett again until her return from San Sebastian. Nor does he see Cohn, who has reportedly gone to the country for a couple of weeks. Upon Brett's return, arrangements are made for everyone to join Jake and his friend, Bill Gorton, on their fishing trip to Spain. Brett worries that this excursion might be rough on Cohn, revealing that they were together in San Sebastian. Jake and Bill meet Cohn in Bayonne and travel on to Pamplona but, at the last minute, Cohn backs out of the fishing trip, deciding instead to meet Brett and Mike in San Sebastian. Jake and Bill spend five days fishing, drinking and playing bridge in Burguete, then return to Pamplona to meet Brett, Mike, and Cohn.

After witnessing the unloading of the bulls, Cohn remarks that "it's no life being a steer." This comment starts Mike, who is drunk and who knows of the affair with Brett, on a long tirade against Cohn. He figures Cohn should enjoy being a steer, since they never say anything and are always hanging about. He asks Cohn why it is that he does not know when he is not wanted and why he follows Brett around like a steer. That night, Jake is unable to sleep. He is jealous of what happened to Cohn. He likes to see Mike hurt him but wishes he would not do it because he feels disgusted with himself afterwards.

On the first day of the fiesta of San Fermin, Jake, Brett and the others are led into a wine shop by a group of men dancing in the street. All eat, drink, sing and have a good time, except Cohn, who passes out in a back room. The following afternoon, Jake and Bill are introduced to Pedro Romero, a young bullfighter. Later, they see that Pedro is a "real one"—his bullfighting gives real emotion whereas the others only fake danger. After the bullfight, Brett says she thinks Pedro lovely and comments on his tight green trousers.

The next morning, Montoya, owner of the hotel where the "real ones" stay, seeks Jake's advice concerning the American ambassador's request to meet Pedro. Montoya fears the influence such a meeting might have on the young bullfighter and Jake agrees that Montoya should not pass along the message. Later that day, Jake finds himself sitting in the dining room with Brett, his friends and Pedro. Montoya enters the room and starts to smile at Jake but then notices Pedro sitting at a table full of drunks. He leaves the room without even nodding.

A little while later, Brett tells Jake that she is mad about Pedro. Jake advises her not to do anything but then agrees to help her find the young bullfighter. When Cohn finds out that Brett and Pedro are together, he calls Jake a pimp and boxes him and Mike to the ground. He then finds Brett and Pedro and beats the bullfighter badly. Later that night, he apologizes to Jake and explains that he could not stand Brett's cool behavior toward him. He tells Jake that he will be leaving in the morning. On the last day of the fiesta, Jake and the others learn that Brett has gone off with Pedro.

Book III

The fiesta over, Jake, Bill and Mike all leave Pamplona. They drive together as far as Bayonne, then go their separate ways. Jake plans a quiet week in San Sebastian but a telegram from Brett shortens his stay. He joins her in Madrid and there learns that she has sent Pedro away. She tells Jake that she realized Pedro should not be living with anyone and that she did not want to be "one of these bitches that ruins children." She then tells him that she will go back to Mike. They arrange for tickets out of Madrid and stop for drinks and dinner. Afterwards, they go for a ride in a taxi. Sitting close to Jake, Brett says: "Oh, Jake, we could have had such a damned good time together." Jake's response ends the novel: "Yes, isn't it pretty to think so?"

Characters

Lady Brett Ashley

Lady Brett Ashley best encapsulates the beauty of being "lost." She represents the dead aristocracy and constantly fends off the long-dead notions of romance best captured in the melancholy of Robert Cohn. Yet she also represents the future and the new feminism of the 1920s; she is an amoral socialite who lost her first love and husband to dysentery in the War, divorced her second because he was abusive but gave her a title, and is working on a third. She is the interesting woman of intelligence from the nineteenth century that Henry James would want to make into a portrait. Lastly, she is an inspiration to otherwise impotent writers because she "was damned good-looking … [and] built like the hull of a racing yacht." Consequent to all these ingredients and the fact that she is in love with Jake, Brett is the moving force of the novel's action. She is also Hemingway's denunciation of all bohemians.

Jake Barnes

The narrator of the story is Jake Barnes. Like his Biblical namesake Jacob, Jake has trouble sleeping because he wrestles nightly with his fate. He is an American living in Paris as a newspaper correspondent. He was rendered impotent by a

World War I wound and is thus unable to consummate his love with Brett. Both his physical condition and his terse manner embody the sterility of the age. Jake forgets the war by immersing himself in the meticulous details of life. He has a calculated view of the events in the story and is sure to relate minutiae, such as how much things cost, who owes whom, how to bait the hook, and what is in the packed lunch. His method for living and being at ease with the world is not unlike the Count's. He states his philosophy, which is the new moral for a world disillusioned by war, as "you paid some way for everything that was any good. I paid my way into enough things that I liked, so that I had a good time. Either you paid by learning about them, or by experience, or by taking chances, or by money. Enjoying living was learning to get your money's worth and knowing when you had it."

Media Adaptations

- Using a screenplay by Peter Viertel, Twentieth Century-Fox adapted *The Sun Also Rises* to the big screen. The movie was released in 1957 and was directed by Harry King. The film stars Tyrone Power, Ava Gardner, and Errol Flynn.

- Directed by James Goldstone and starring Elisabeth Borgnine, *The Sun Also Rises* was adapted for television in 1985.

Jake Barnes is Hemingway's first and best attempt to explain to others the mannerisms which enable constructive living with an accompanying disillusionment. Exaggerating this position, Jake is a man to whom things happen. Through no fault of his own, he was a victim of war; he suffers a wound that prevents a normal life. His story is an effort, not so much to react to the world, but to sort out in a visible manner an explanation for his life and a solution to his quandary. He discovers a coded style of "hardboiledness" which he uses to pull off the appearance of living with the war. Along with this, he turns to the relational exchanges embodied in money as his emotional salve. Consequently, his meticulous record of what is spent and how is a reassurance. He grows less and less troubled as he perfects his code among those who are more lost, get less for their money, and are not wounded. Only the Count (who also has physical scars) has an understanding of this and, therefore, he is the only other character who does not appear troubled.

Belmonte

An historical figure, Belmonte was one of the greatest matadors of all time. He is shown in the story as aging and past his prime. This is ironic in the extreme since it is the matador who fulfills the ideal of the hero. Yet, showing a hero in decline makes him all the more human. Belmonte, despite his pain, maintains his dignified poise and provides yet another example of the novel's moral: no matter how you choose to live in this senseless world, live with style.

Mrs. Braddocks

Mrs. Braddocks "was a Canadian and had all their easy social graces." She is attempting to revive pre-war dancing events. At the moment she simply gathers people about her for dinner before they go on their nightly clubbing.

Brett

See Lady Brett Ashley

Michael Campbell

A bankrupt Scotsman who is engaged to Brett, Mike Campbell grows weary of Cohn always hanging around Brett. He takes advantage of Cohn's inferiority complex to needle him. He is made painfully aware that Brett does not love him when she goes off with the matador.

Frances Clyne

Frances believes that she is in love with Cohn. She is ready to sacrifice anything to be with him. Cohn, in his new success as a novelist, would rather seek adventure. Realizing that Cohn has no intention of marrying her, she insults him and leaves for England.

Robert Cohn

The novel opens with Robert Cohn, a mediocre writer and middleweight boxing champion at Princeton with a "hard, Jewish, stubborn streak." He is the representation of all that was supposedly destroyed in the war. Therefore, he must be exiled from the group that is busily reshaping the world.

He is a friend and tennis partner to Jake. Born rich and married rich, he was unhappy until his wife left him. Now free, he decides to pursue happiness in the form of editing a magazine. But when that fails, he moves to Paris with his assistant, Frances, and writes. The success of his first novel goes straight to his head as he lives out his dreams of chivalry and romance; Frances becomes his mistress. From this point, his role is one of decline in the eyes of his associates for, as Brett says, he is not "one of us." From the moment of Brett's judgment, the other men seek ways of being rid of him. Jake succeeds by letting Cohn exile himself.

Cohn's love for Brett and his expression of that love is meant as criticism of the romantic. He represents the American values of love, idealism, and naive bliss that were soundly exploded in World War I. Therefore, Cohn is Hemingway's satirical portrait of the last knight who would defend the old faith and ideals. This knight absurdly undergoes overt humiliation under the guise of a love for a lady and brings upon himself verbal wrath and abuse. Cohn's actions are the last gasp of those values yet his survival is a bitter reminder of their beauty in not too dissimilar ways from Jake's more physical reminder in the form of his wound.

Bill Gorton

One of the few positive characters in the novel arrives in Paris at the start of Book II. Bill Gorton has come to accompany Jake on a fishing expedition but finds he must also buoy his friend's spirits. Bill believes in "a simple exchange of values" and living for the moment. This philosophy prompts him to say, in sight of something that would bring ease, "let's utilize it."

Georgette Hobin

See Georgette Leblanc

Georgette Leblanc

A prostitute, Georgette Leblanc is very cynical and does her utmost to hide her defect—her teeth. She shares a knowledge with Jake that everyone is "sick" in their way but she is not brought into the group.

Count Mippipopolous

The Count has a very simple philosophy of life —get your money's worth and know when you have. He owns a chain of sweet shops and is charmed by Lady Brett, who thinks he is one of them. The Count knows through experience and age what the others are trying to figure out—how to live well.

Montoya

Montoya is the owner of a hotel in Pamplona where Jake habitually stays while in town for the fiesta. He recognizes that Jake is a fellow aficionado —one who is capable of appreciating the ritual bullfight. He is the truest devotee of bullfighting and all the matadors try to stay in his hotel. Montoya does what he can for those matadors who show promise as the "real thing."

Pedro Romero

The stock hero of the tale, Romero is handsome and brave. His beating at the hands of the annoying boxer, Cohn, shows him to be just a man who has a talent for bullfighting.

Themes

Morals and Morality

Reflecting on his friends and especially on Robert Cohn, who is becoming a major annoyance, Jake reflects on his moral code, "That was morality; things that made you disgusted afterward. No, that must be immorality." Jake is more interested in his own concerns and, secondarily, Brett's. Cohn was fortunate enough to have a holiday with Brett but he is not smart enough to accept that it meant nothing. Because Cohn cannot create his own version of the group's code, he becomes the subject of persecution. Jake is bothered by it but he is more disgusted when he knowingly violates the code of aficionado by setting up Brett with Romero. This disrupts his friendship with Montoya and with Cohn. Respect is betrayed and lost. The garbage that is visible at the end of the fiesta only compounds his self-disgust. However, instead of leading to an epiphany he simply decides to develop his own code of style more thoroughly. That style is a hard-boiled self-centeredness.

Brett is lost throughout the novel. She is disgusted with herself and those around her, especially Jake—through no fault of his own. The only moment she exerts herself in terms of morality is to get rid of Romero. Throughout the novel, Brett defies conventional morality by having short, meaningless affairs. Because of her self-centeredness and unhappiness, she is unable to stop this self-destructive behavior and is often passive to events. The affairs are meant to escape her unsatisfactory relationship with Jake, whom she truly loves but who is unable to physically consummate their relationship.

Meaning of Life

The theme of life's meaning turns from the question of essence, "what it was all about," to existence, "how to live in it." However, the reason for this polarity is the inability of the main characters to rise above that mediocrity. They must reject the life of the hero as impossible for themselves. "Nobody ever lives their life all the way up except bullfighters." To which Cohn replies, "I am not interested in bullfighters. That's an abnormal life." Cohn's idea of life is romantic—a life of literary fame and adventure with a beautiful mistress who happens to have a title. But the group despises Cohn's notions and Brett finally judges that he is "not one of us." Instead, the key to life is a development of one's ability to wisely utilize the full worth of one's money. This can take many forms but only Jake, the Count, and to a certain extent Bill Gorton, are able to do this. Brett, and especially Mike Campbell (who is ever an "undischarged bankrupt"), will never be happy even if they become rich because they are incapable of utilizing money well.

Bill relies on exchange value and use. When he first enters the narrative he wishes to buy Jake a stuffed dog, "Simple exchange of values. You give them money. They give you a stuffed dog." Bill's philosophy is to use money to buy moments as well as to show one's stature. His motto is "Never be daunted." Possibilities for bliss, such as a pub or a bottle, must be utilized to their full potential.

Topics for Further Study

- After doing some research on bullfighting and its surrounding festival, explain the novel according to your findings discussing whether or not the British title of *Fiesta* was more or less appropriate. Is the bullfight the focus of the novel? Back up your claims by examining each character's reaction to the spectacle.

- Thinking about the role that the matador plays in the novel, what is the role of a hero in a world disillusioned by war? Would you agree with cultural anthropologist Joseph Campbell that his role (and Joseph Campbell does emphasize the need for rejuvenating masculine heroic ritual) is to reconnect people into a "coordinated soul"? As he says in *The Hero with a Thousand Faces*, "It is not society that is to guide and save the creative hero, but precisely the reverse." Lastly, do you think Hemingway was working with this idea in mind?

- Compare *The Sun Also Rises* with Jack Kerouac's *On the Road*. How does the spokesman for the "lost generation" compare with that of the "beat generation"?

- Given the conditions of agrarian life in the dust bowl of the early part of this century, what arguments can you make for linking the "greats" of the "lost generation" to their birth-region? Except for Ezra Pound (Idaho), they are all from the Midwest—F. Scott Fitzgerald (MN), Ernest Hemingway (IL), Sherwood Anderson (OH), Sinclair Lewis (MN), and T.S. Eliot (MO).

- Would Hemingway, or any character in his novel, approve of a female matador? Provide evidence from the novel or from other Hemingway novels or short fiction to support your assertion.

Jake, meanwhile, is developing a more sophisticated attitude full of tabulating expenses which keeps his mind off his main problem of impotence. "I paid my way into things that I liked, so that I had a good time. Either you paid by learning about them or by experience, or by taking chances, or by money. Enjoying living was learning to get your money's worth and knowing when you had it. You could get your money's worth. The world was a good place to buy in." Then he adds that he might change his mind in five years. In other words, "the lost generation" can get their kicks by a wise expenditure of money (even if they are not rich) until a semblance of reality has been reconstructed and the war is in the past. A possible future philosophy is hinted at when Jake reads Turgenieff and knows he will remember what he reads as if it was his experience. That is, Turgenieff writes truthfully about experience in a way Hemingway agreed with. "That was another good thing you paid for and then had." But payment here is the effort of reading literature which you can then use to recover from war.

Narrative

The first-person narration of Jake Barnes is sometimes referred to as a "roman à clef." A roman à clef is a story understandable only to those who have a "key" for deciphering the real persons and places behind the story. The story of Jake Barnes resembles the real events of the summer of 1925 in the life of Hemingway and his friends. Still there is enough difference that no "key" is needed for understanding. That is to say, the novel stands on its own whether or not the reader knows on whom the character Lady Brett Ashley is based. In addition, Jake Barnes is not Hemingway because in real life Hemingway was married when he went to Pamplona. Jake is a blending of several real people as well as a fruition of Hemingway's theoretic code-hero. There is enough similarity for comparisons but the novel is in no way an autobiographical event. It is a story attempting to speak truths to the present generation.

Dialogue

Hemingway's dependence on dialogue is just one mark of his modernity. Henry James, for example, felt dialogue was the climax of a scene and was to be used sparingly. Hemingway creates whole scenes solely from dialogue. However,

Hemingway's dialogue made the story an easy and fast read with effects similar to news writing. The author seems to disappear as the narrator allows his contact with others to balance out the story. It becomes a group conversation rather than a narration. Hemingway's ability with this feature delighted many critics. Conrad Aiken remarked, "More than any other talk I can call to mind, it is alive with the rhythms and idioms, the pauses and suspensions and innuendoes and shorthands, of living speech. It is in the dialogue, almost entirely, that Mr. Hemingway tells his story and makes the people live and act." The use of dialogue is one of the key features of Hemingway's style.

Hero

Hemingway's solution to the ennui, or disillusioned nausea, that marked his "lost generation" was the encouragement of each person in their path to being a hero. However, as is clear in the novel, his theory did not include bravery in war or sport but insisted that the individual create a moral code. One must "never be daunted."

Jake Barnes and friends are the best examples of Hemingway pursuing his theories. Succeeding Hemingway heroes do have the humanity to inspire our sympathy and imitation. This code-hero was defined eloquently by Robert Penn Warren and Cleanth Brooks while discussing Hemingway's "The Killers." They said that the code-hero "is the tough man,… the disciplined man, who actually is aware of pathos or tragedy." Lacking spontaneous emotion, the code-hero "sheathes [his sensibility] in the code of toughness" because "he has learned that the only way to hold on to 'honor,' to individuality, to, even, the human order … is to live by his code." Romero provides the clearest example not through his bullfighting but through his ability to ignore the bruises Cohn gives him in order to perform as he is capable. The success of the fiesta depends on his ability to do so. Brett and Jake also satisfy this definition. Brett decides she cannot corrupt the young bullfighter but will continue to live in style hiding her frustrated love. Jake decides he has to live according to his own code with the help of his stoicism.

Idiom

The heavy use of dialogue, the terse, staccato sentences, and the minimalist tightness that characterizes descriptions and emotional expenditure are the marks of the style or idiom that Hemingway made his own. According to this idiom, carefully chosen language can relate fictional authenticity in such a way that it will never ring false, the goal being to carefully construct a world that has certitude and leave the uncertain unsaid. Thus the language appears often to refer to ideas beyond what is actually written. However, only the written words are to be trusted and only they are true. The effect of this new style is similar to Biblical genesis: reconstruct from the rubble of war a civilization of beauty and simplicity.

The bareness of the intention is best revealed on the fishing expedition. "Once in the night I woke and heard the wind blowing. It felt good to be warm and in bed." Two sentences were used where previous writers would have expended chapters. Furthermore, it is an incredibly simple and stark contrast to the sleepless nights of Paris and it directly calls to mind the howls of the "Waste Land."

The Lost Generation

Writers, horrified by the stranglehold of business and the uselessness of Prohibition, expatriated to Paris where the favorable exchange rate enabled them to work for a newspaper or magazine. Yet these writers usually spent most of their time sitting in cafes lost in the aftermath of a war for which they refused responsibility. Disillusioned, they discussed their inherited nineteenth-century values and the provincial and emotional barrenness of America. Fortunately, they found comfort in an older generation. Hemingway, armed with letters of introduction by Sherwood Anderson, joined this group who flocked to Gertrude Stein's Salon, Sylvia Beach's Shakespeare and Company book-store, the apartment of James Joyce, *the transatlantic review* offices of Ford Madox Ford, or Samuel Putnam's office. The older writers cultivated the members of what Stein labeled, after overhearing her mechanic, as "the lost generation." Of the elders Stein, who was the bridge between past and present, and Ezra Pound, whom Hemingway tried to teach boxing in return for tutelage, were the most important influences on Hemingway.

"The Lost Generation" succeeded in poking through the rubble of civilization and manufacturing art anew. From war's negation comes affirmation as a means to live with disillusionment. T.S. Eliot wove the old myths together into a poem of epic influence, "The Waste Land." A new poetry was created by e.e. cummings. F. Scott Fitzgerald, John Dos Passos, Hart Crane, and Glenway Westcott were members of this generation who helped rejuvenate the arts. The most important contribution of "The Lost Generation" was to prove the resiliency of culture and set it moving again with the hopeful idealism that would mark American literature in the 1930s.

The Roaring Twenties

In the Europe of the mid-1920s, life was returning to normal and cities were being reconstructed after the devastation of World War I. Tensions, which still existed between France and Germany over border issues, were quiet, as France became isolated. The French war effort had depended on American loans and their repayment depended on reparations from Germany. These reparations were recovered with difficulty because Britain and the United States were hesitant to force matters. Still, Germany was potentially the most powerful nation in Europe and was quietly being given favorable loan terms by the United States. The French economy worsened when the franc was stabilized at 20% of its pre war value. This had the effect of making France a collector of gold and brought adventure-seeking Americans, with moderate sums of dollars, to take advantage of exchange rates.

New Leaders

Though a long way off, the leaders who would play a large role in World War II came to power. Josef Stalin assumed his 27-year dictatorship in the Soviet Union. He de-emphasized world revolution in favor of repressing and terrorizing Soviet citizens and Russian neighbors. The Politburo, meanwhile, expelled Leon Trotsky and Grigori Zinoviev. In Italy, Benito Mussolini assumed control of the country and the Fascist party became the party of state without opposition. Chiang Kai-shek succeeded Sun Yat-Sen and began to unify China. In Japan, Yoshihito died and his son became Emperor Hirohito (a role which he retained until his death in 1989).

Compare & Contrast

- **1920s:** Thomas Hunt Morgan proves his theory of hereditary transmission through experiments with fruit flies and publishes *The Theory of the Gene* in 1926. Coincidentally, Herman Joseph Mullar proves that X-rays can produce genetic mutations.

  Today: It is no longer speculation that genes provide the source code for life and can be mutated by radiation. In fact, Morgan's ground-breaking experiment is now an exercise in college biology rooms. Moreover, armed with lessons in genetic engineering, biotechnology firms are literally changing the fabric of nature by gene manipulation and the techniques of cloning.

- **1920s:** The "Noble Experiment" of Prohibition is in full swing. Backers hope it will make America better by forcing its people to be sober. Instead, average citizens flout the law by patronizing illegal establishments run by the Mafia. Bootlegging is a billion-dollar industry.
  Today: The "War on Drugs" is mounted to stop the sale of hard drugs and urban deterioration in the United States.

- **1920s:** The tuna industry is in a crisis as albacore disappears off the California coast. The industry begins harvesting the lower quality yellow-fin tuna.
  Today: The entire fishing industry is in a crisis with vast areas of the oceans fished out. Whole strata of the aquatic food chain have disappeared with lower-level fish,

like jellyfish, producing record numbers for lack of predators. The situation is so bad that normally friendly nations (like Great Britain, Canada, Spain, and Portugal) have almost come to blows over fishing rights.

- **1920s:** The Spanish ritual of bullfighting is confined to Spain and parts of Latin America. It is purely a male domain.

  Today: The popularity of bullfighting continues to rise and many Americans venture to Pamplona for the bull run. There have been several female matadors and recently a female champion.

Economics

For members of the upper middle class or the rich, the twenties were indeed the era of prosperity, debauchery, and bootlegging. For the rest of humanity, life was still a struggle. The 1921 musical "Ain't We Got Fun" encapsulates the period saying, "The rich get richer, and the poor get children." Coal miners in America stretched their meager 75-cents-per-hour wages (roughly $7.50 in 1995 dollars) to feed their families. Public-school teachers made slightly less at $1000 a year. Labor movements were met with brutal force but there were few improvements. The Ford Motor Company introduced an 8-hour day and a 5-day week. The picture for blacks in America was especially hard with 85% of blacks living in the segregated south and 23% of them illiterate. Great numbers of blacks began migrating north to the cities with lasting demographic effects.

Meanwhile, labor relations in Britain were tantamount to class war. A general strike crippled the nation as coal miners belonging to the Trade Union Congress demanded, "Not a penny off the pay; not a minute on the day." Many workers sympathetic to the miners (railwaymen, printers, dockworkers, construction workers, and others) went on strike as well. At the root of the problem was the decision by Chancellor of the Exchequer Winston Churchill to return to the gold standard. That decision had the effect of cheapening import prices and thus forcing mine operators to cut wages so as to compete with German and Polish imports. Economist John Maynard Keynes considered Churchill's decision "silly." Matters nearly erupted in violence as the Royal Navy trained its guns on strikers who tried to prevent the off-loading of ships at the docks.

Critical Overview

Already prepared for his style by the short story collection *In Our Time* and the subject matter by a short story, "The Undefeated," Hemingway's readers asserted that *The Sun Also Rises* more than satisfied expectations. The novel was appreciated for its modern "ease" and quickly became the novel of the "lost generation." More recently, the novel has helped rejuvenate Hemingway's reputation. Critical attention to the novel can categorized as follows: early surprise and discussion of plot (focusing on the bullfighting, Europe, or "the lost generation"); the alternative morality Hemingway provides in the face of disillusionment; the facts of impotency and gender in the novel; and finally, where the novel fits into Hemingway's reputation.

Except for Allen Tate's, the first reviews were glowing, congratulatory, and painfully aware of the ubiquitous war fatigue. Conrad Aiken, in the *New York Herald Tribune*, was struck first and foremost by the bullfighting which he compared to "half a course of psycho-analysis." "One is thrilled and horrified; but one is also fascinated, and one cannot have enough." Aiken observes that the novel "works up to, and in a sense is built around, a bullfight." In addition, he is unaware of anyone using dialogue better than Hemingway does. A reviewer for the *New York Times Book Review* said, "It is a truly gripping story, told in a lean, hard, athletic narrative prose that puts mere literary English to shame.

Hemingway knows how ... to arrange a collection of words which shall betray a great deal more than is to be found in the individual parts." Lawrence S. Morris, in *The New Republic*, saw the novel as "one stride toward that objectification" which the current generation needed after rejecting its inherited myths. Tate wrote negatively, in *The Nation*, that the significance of Hemingway's subject matter "is mixed or incomplete." Furthermore, the habit of throwing stones at the great "is disconcerting in the present novel; it strains the context; and one suspects that Mr. Hemingway protests too much. The point he seems to be making is that he is morally superior ... [to] Mr. Mencken, but it is not yet clear just why."

James T. Farrell wrote a 1943 reaction, in the *New York Times*, to a novel that was supposedly "the definite account of a war-wearied lost generation." He explained the novel's popularity as a result of the pacifism of the post-war generation ready to challenge those values that had brought that war. Hemingway's novel, therefore, was right on time. "He arrived on the literary scene the absolute master of the style he has made his own; his attitudes were firmly fixed at that time, and he said pretty much what he had to say with his first stories, and his first two novels." Philip Young was more succinct, saying the novel is "still Hemingway's *Waste Land* and Jake is Hemingway's Fisher King."

Criticism became more analytical through the 1950s and gradually dissected Hemingway the man.

Mark Spilka, in *Twelve Original Essays*, tried to find the moral of the story by focusing on its love theme. He concluded that Pedro is the hero of the story. Therefore, the lesson is that a hero is someone "whose code gives meaning to a world where love and religion are defunct." Carlos Baker focused on the geography because "place and the sense of fact … [as well as the] operation of the sense of scene" is Hemingway's style, nothing more. Earl H. Rovit felt otherwise, in *Landmarks of American Writing*. He likened the novel to a "Newtonian world-machine" which rendered the metaphor of our age —which is explosion—conscious for the first time. For this reason the novel continues to "provoke our thought." Terrence Doody, in *The Journal of Narrative Technique*, was moved to say Hemingway did not know what he was doing with his narrator Jake Barnes. He added that the "naive contact with the world" the Hemingway style enables is clearly not sufficient since Faulkner and Fitzgerald are now preferred.

Sam S. Baskett picked up on the debate over Jake Barnes for his review in *The Centennial Review*, asking what sort of moral center Hemingway, spokesman for a generation, had come up with. Baskett answered this question by noting the value that characters have for themselves is a function of their regard for Brett—their godhead. Thus, Jake is the hero because he understands how to "live as a moral being" through writing his story and ignoring Brett. Andrew Hook's review, in *Ernest Hemingway: New Critical Essays*, is also interested in the moral center which is imposed, contrary to the novels that follow where the hero makes the choice, on Jake. Hook found that in this novel Hemingway "risks challenging the very codes and values" of the rest of his fiction and his life.

Criticism of the 1980s summed up Hemingway or discussed issues of gender. Nina Schwartz, in *Criticism*, analyzed the novel as an attempt to return "man to the center of a humanistic universe" by allowing Jake to control the signifiers. The crucial act here is Jake's displacement of his own desire to his favorite hero, Romero. Woman, or Brett as love object, assumes the most powerful position as castrator of "the very mythos of castration." The woman becomes the author of the men and the Bull of their ritual. Sukrita Paul Kumar more simply declared woman as the hero of the novel, not Jake or Romero. Kumar said the novel "paves the way for complete androgynous relationships through an acceptance and absorption of the new values as well as the new female ideal." Sibbie O'Sullivan's article, in *Arizona Quarterly*, defended Hemingway against charges of misogyny: he respected the new woman being created in the 1920s. O'Sullivan took inspiration from Jake's idea that you had to love a woman to befriend her and showed that Brett "is a positive force ... who makes an attempt to live honestly."

Lastly, John W. Aldridge summarized up Hemingway's modern reputation in *The Sewanee Review*. The dark side of the author is forgiven and his first novel is held up as a continuing inspiration for us not to "give up [our] hold on the basic sanities."

Sources

Conrad Aiken, "Expatriates," in *New York Herald Tribune Books*, October 31, 1926, p. 4.

John W. Aldridge, *"The Sun Also Rises*—Sixty Years Later," in *The Sewanee Review*, Vol. XCIV, No. 2, Spring, 1986, pp. 337-45.

Carlos Baker, in *Hemingway: The Writer as Artist*, third edition, Princeton University Press, 1963, p. 379.

Sam S. Baskett, "'An Image to Dance Around': Brett and Her Lovers in *'The Sun Also Rises'"* in *The Centennial Review*, Vol. XXII, No. 1, Winter, 1978, pp. 45-69.

Cleanth Brooks Jr. and Robert Penn Warren, " *'The Killers'*, Ernest Hemingway: Interpretation," in *Understanding Fiction*, edited by Cleanth Brooks, Jr. and Robert Penn Warren, Appleton-Century-Crofts, Inc., 1959, pp. 306-25.

Terrence Doody, "Hemingway's Style and Jake's Narration," in *The Journal of Narrative Technique*, Vol. 4, No. 3, September, 1974, pp. 212-25.

James T. Farrell, "Ernest Hemingway, Apostle of a 'Lost Generation'," in *The New York Times Books Review*, August 1, 1943, pp. 6, 14.

Andrew Hook, "Art and Life in *The Sun Also Rises,"* in *Ernest Hemingway: New Critical Essays*, edited by A. Robert Lee, Vision Press, 1983, pp. 49-

63.

Sukrita Paul Kumar, "Woman as Hero in Hemingway's *The Sun Also Rises,"* in *The Literary Endeavour*, Vol. VI, Nos. 1-4, 1985, pp. 102-08.

"Marital Tragedy," in *The New York Times Book Review*, October 31, 1926, p. 7.

Lawrence S. Morris, "Warfare in Man and among Men," in *The New Republic*, Vol. XLIX, No. 629, December 22,1926, pp. 142-43.

Sibbie O'Sullivan, "Love and Friendship/Man and Woman in *The Sun Also Rises,"* in *Arizona Quarterly*, Vol. 44, No. 2, Summer, 1988, pp. 76-97.

Earl H. Rovit, "Ernest Hemingway: *The Sun Also Rises,"* in *Landmarks of American Writing*, edited by Hennig Cohen, Basic Books, Inc., 1969, pp. 303-14.

Nina Schwartz, "Lovers' Discourse in *The Sun Also Rises:* A Cock and Bull Story," in *Criticism*, Vol. XXVI, No. 1, Winter, 1984, pp. 49-69.

Mark Spilka, "The Death of Love in *The Sun Also Rises,"* in *Twelve Original Essays on Great American Novels*, edited by Charles Shapiro, Wayne State University Press, 1958, pp. 238-56.

Allen Tate, "Hard Boiled," in *The Nation*, Vol. CXXIII, No. 3206, December 15, 1926, pp. 642, 644.

Phillip Young, in *Ernest Hemingway*, Rinehart & Company, Inc., 1952, p. 244.

For Further Study

Donald A. Daiker, "The Affirmative Conclusion of *The Sun Also Rises,"* in *Modern American Fiction: Form and Function*, edited by Thomas Daniel Young, Louisiana State University Press, 1989, pp. 39-56.

> Daiker asserts that a close reading of Book III reveals that *The Sun Also Rises* is an affimnative book.

Scott Donaldson, "Humor in *The Sun Also Rises,"* in *New Essays on* The Sun Also Rises, edited by Linda Wagner-Martin, Cambridge University Press, 1987, pp. 19-41.

> Revealing that Hemingway started his writing career trying to be funny, Donaldson discusses the author's use of humor in *The Sun Also Rises.*

Barry Gross, "Dealing with Robert Cohn," in *Hemingway in Italy and Other Essays*, edited by Robert W. Lewis, Praeger, 1990, pp. 123-30.

> Gross discusses the depiction of Robert Cohn and the issue of anti-Semitism in *The Sun Also Rises.*

Robert E. Flemming, "The Importance of Count Mippipopolous. Creating the Code Hero," in *Arizona Quarterly*, Vol. 44, No. 2, Summer, 1988, pp. 69-75.

> Flemming contends that the Count may be an early prototype in Hemingway's fiction of the character type known as the "code hero."

Ernest Hemingway, in *Death in the Afternoon*, Touchstone Books, 1996.

> Contains Hemingway's own discussion of his favorite sport—bullfighting. The book explains the ritual and provides pictures.

Allen, Josephs, 'Toreo: The Moral Axis of *The Sun Also Rises,"* in *Critical Essays on Ernest Hemingway's* The Sun Also Rises, edited by James Nagel, G.K. Hall & Co., 1995, pp. 126-40.

> Josephs explores how and why the art of *toreo* lies at the heart of *The Sun Also Rises.*

Albert Kwan, *"The Sun Also Rises* and *On the Road,"* at http://www.atlantic.net/~gagne/pol/ontheroad.html, 1998.

> World War II created a group of artists with similar disillusions to those of the Lost Generation. This group came to be know as the Beat Generation and in Albert Kwan's essay Ernest Hemingway and Jack Kerouac are compared.

Kenneth S. Lynn, in *Hemingway*, Fawcett Books, 1988.

> In an attempt to be objective about

Hemingway, Kenneth Lynn is seen by some fans as a bit harsh in this biographical account. It is an unusually balanced work for a Hemingway biography and it is not afraid to reveal some of the darker things about the famous writer.

James Nagel, "Brett and the Other Women in 'The Sun Also Rises'," in *The Cambridge Companion to Hemingway*, edited by Scott Donaldson, Cambridge University Press, 1996, pp. 87-108.

In this discussion of the women in *The Sun Also Rises*, Nagel agues that, in order to come to terms with his emotional devastation, Jake tells his story—a cathartic reiteration that focuses on Brett and the women who surround her.

Kathleen Nichols, "The Morality of Asceticism in *The Sun Also Rises:* A Structural Reinterpretation," in *Fitzgerald/Hemingway Annual*, edited by Matthew J. Bruccoli and Richard Layman, 1978, pp. 321-30.

Nichols contends that the solution Jake finds to his problems might be called a secularized morality based on the Catholic ideal of asceticism.

Sibbie O'Sullivan, "Love and Friendship/Man and Woman in *The Sun Also Rises,"* in *Arizona Quarterly*, Vol. 44, 1988, pp. 76-97.

O'Sullivan proposes that the novel may be read as a story about the cautious belief in the survival of the two most basic components of any human relationship: love and friendship.

Michael S. Reynolds, "The Sun in Its Time: Recovering the Historical Context," in *New Essays on* The Sun Also Rises, edited by Linda Wagner-Martin, Cambridge University Press, 1987, pp. 43-64.

Arguing that *The Sun Also Rises* is "anchored in time," Reynolds places the novel in its historical context.

—, in *The Sun Also Rises: A Novel of the Twenties*, Twayne Publishers, 1988.

A book-length study of the themes, characters, and symbolism of the novel.

Linda Wagner-Martin, "Introduction," in *New Essays on 'The Sun Also Rises'*, edited by Linda Wagner-Martin, Cambridge University Press, 1987, pp. 1-18.

Wagner-Martin discusses various biographical, historical and textual issues in this introduction to a volume of essays on *The Sun Also Rises.*

Jane E. Wilson, "Good Old Harris in *The Sun Also Rises,"* in *Critical Essays on Ernest Hemingway's*

The Sun Also Rises, edited by James Nagel, G.K. Hall & Co., 1995, pp. 185-90.

> Wilson discusses the fishing trip to Burguete and argues that Jake's relationship with Harris is the key to understanding the meaning of the episode.

Milton Keynes UK
Ingram Content Group UK Ltd.
UKHW032316121024
449481UK00011B/314